Sheep

Quinn M. Arnold

CREATIVE EDUCATION • CREATIVE PAPERBACKS

seedlings

Published by Creative Education and Creative Paperbacks
P.O. Box 227, Mankato, Minnesota 56002
Creative Education and Creative Paperbacks
are imprints of The Creative Company
www.thecreativecompany.us

Design by Ellen Huber; production by Joe Kahnke
Art direction by Rita Marshall
Printed in the United States of America

Photographs by Alamy (Art Directors & TRIP, Rosemary Harris,
Wayne HUTCHINSON, Ernie Janes), Dreamstime (Innaastakhova,
Isselee, Khunaspix, Walter Kopplinger, Nathan Mcclunie, Thomas
Payne, Bernhard Richter, Fesus Robert, Timbooth2770), Getty
Images (Nigel Roddis), iStockphoto (Barcin, grahamsimage),
Shutterstock (dreamloveyou, Phil.Tinkler)

Library of Congress Cataloging-in-Publication Data
Arnold, Quinn M.
Sheep / Quinn M. Arnold.
p. cm. — (Seedlings)
Includes bibliographical references and index.
Summary: A kindergarten-level introduction to sheep,
covering their growth process, behaviors, the farms they call
home, and such defining features as their woolly fleece.
ISBN 978-1-60818-788-1 (hardcover)
ISBN 978-1-62832-396-2 (pbk)
ISBN 978-1-56660-830-5 (eBook)
This title has been submitted for
CIP processing under LCCN 2016937135.

CCSS: RI.K.1, 2, 3, 4, 5, 6, 7;
RI.1.1, 2, 3, 4, 5, 6, 7; RF.K.1, 3; RF.1.1

First Edition HC 9 8 7 6 5 4 3 2 1
First Edition PBK 9 8 7 6 5 4 3 2 1

TABLE OF CONTENTS

Hello, sheep!

Many sheep live on farms. Some farms have only a few sheep. Others have large flocks.

A sheep's fleece is wool. It can be white, gray, black, or brown.

It is cut every spring to help the sheep stay cool.

Sheep have excellent hearing and eyesight. Their big ears turn toward sounds.

Rectangular pupils help sheep see.

Sheep graze in fields. They eat grasses and leafy plants. Some farmers feed sheep hay or grains.

Lambs are baby sheep.
First they drink milk.
Then they eat grasses
and grains. Lambs
run and play together.

They climb on top
of other sheep.

Sheep eat and nap.

Sheepdogs help keep the flock safe.

17

Goodbye, sheep!

Picture a Sheep

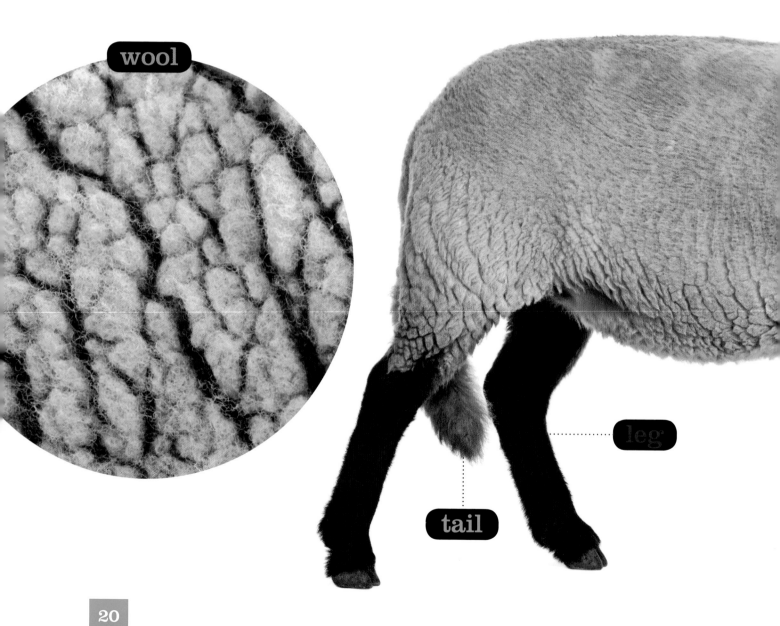

wool

leg

tail

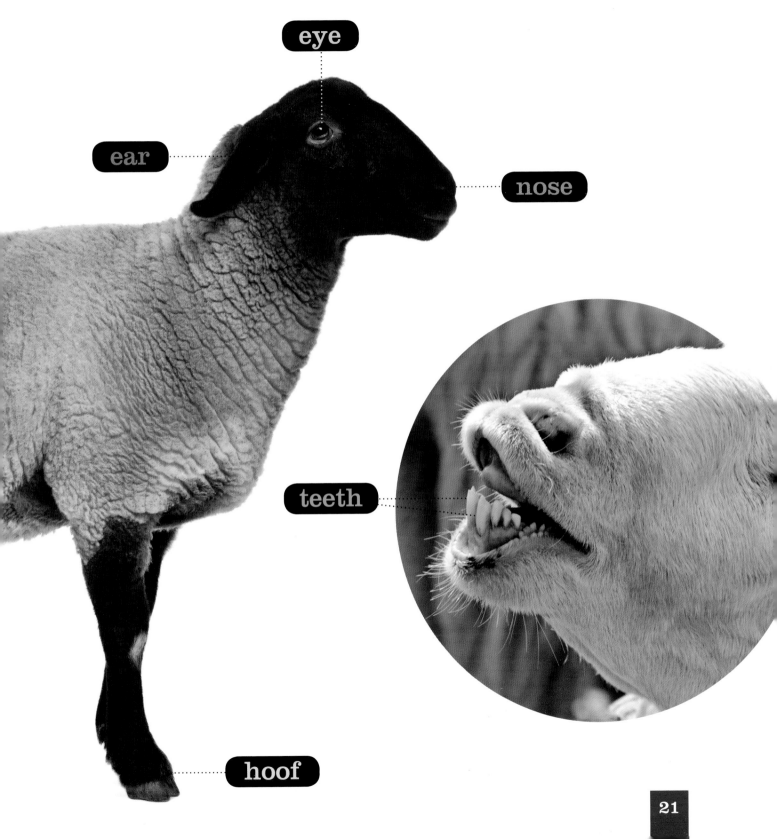

eye

ear

nose

teeth

hoof

Words to Know

fleece: the woolly coat of a sheep; people use wool to make clothes and blankets

flocks: numbers of sheep that are kept together

graze: to feed on grasses in an open area

pupils: the middle of the eyes that allow light to enter, enabling vision

Read More

Dieker, Wendy Strobel. *Sheep.*
Minneapolis: Jump!, 2013.

Wendorff, Anne. *Lambs.*
Minneapolis: Bellwether Media, 2014.

Websites

DLTK's Lamb or Sheep Coloring Pages
http://www.coloring.ws/lambs.htm
Print out a picture of a lamb or sheep to color.

The Kid's Fun Review: March Lamb Craft
http://kidsfunreviewed.com/march-lamb-craft/
Use construction paper, cotton balls, and twigs to
make your own sheep.

Index